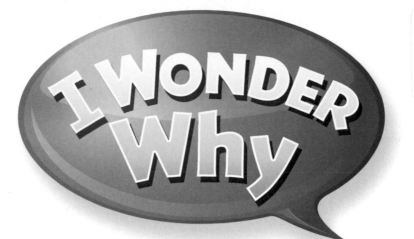

Mountains
Have Snow on Top

and other questions
about mountains

Jackie Gaff

KINGFISHER
NEW YORK

KINGFISHER
LONDON & NEW YORK

Copyright © Macmillan Publishers International Ltd 2012
Published in the United States by Kingfisher,
175 Fifth Ave., New York, NY 10010
Kingfisher is an imprint of Macmillan Children's Books,
London.
All rights reserved.

First published 2001 by Kingfisher
This edition published 2017 by Kingfisher

Consultant: Keith Lye

Distributed in the U.S. and Canada by Macmillan,
175 Fifth Ave., New York, NY 10010

Library of Congress Cataloging-in-Publication data
has been applied for.

ISBN 978-0-7534-6700-8 (HC)
ISBN 978-0-7534-7361-0 (PB)

Kingfisher books are available for special promotions and
premiums. For details contact: Special Markets Department,
Macmillan, 175 Fifth Avenue, New York, NY 10010.

For more information, please visit www.kingfisherbooks.com

Printed in China
9 8 7 6 5 4 3 2 1
1TR/0716/WKT/UNTD/128MA

Illustrations: Mark Bergin 28b, 31b; James Field (SGA) 20t,
22–23, 24t; Mike Lacey (SGA) 4, 8–9, 20b, 21t, 23b, 24–25,
26–27, 29, 30; Sean Milne 18–19; Liz Sawyer (SGA) 16–17,
19b; Stephen Sweet (SGA) 6–7, 8t; Mike Taylor (SGA) 12–13;
Ross Walton (SGA) 5, 10–11, 14–15, 28–29, 30–31; Peter
Wilkes (SGA) all cartoons.

Cover: A golden eagle flies over snow capped peaks near
Denali, Alaska.

CONTENTS

What's the difference between a mountain and a hill?

Mountains are larger than hills, and mountainsides are often steep and tough to climb—unlike a hill's gentle slopes. Some experts say that if a peak is more than 2,000 feet (600m) higher than the surrounding land, then it is a mountain. Any less, it is a hill.

About one-fourth of all land on Earth is mountainous.

A row of mountains is called a range.

Can spacecraft measure mountains?

Radar equipment is used to measure mountains by bouncing sound signals off the ground. Machines record the time the signals take to bounce back and then use this to figure out how high a mountain is. The radar is carried onboard high-flying airplanes and space satellites.

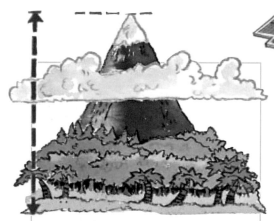

Even though a mountain may be a long way from the ocean, its height is figured as the distance above the ocean's surface—sea level.

The top of a mountain is called its peak or summit.

Where is the world's highest mountain?

The highest place in the whole world is at the top of Mount Everest. This huge mountain is in the Himalayan ranges of central Asia, and it rises to 29,029 feet (8,848m) above sea level.

Although only 13,796 feet (4,205m) of Mauna Kea sticks up above sea level, this Hawaiian mountain is even taller than Everest. From its base on the ocean floor to its peak, Mauna Kea is an amazing 33,474 feet (10,203m).

The world's longest mountain range on land is the Andes in South America, at about 4,500 miles (7,200km) long.

NORTH AMERICA

Alaska Range

Rocky Mountains

Appalachians

Sierra Nevada

ATLANTIC OCEAN

SOUTH AMERICA

Andes

Famous mountains

① **Denali**
20,308 ft.
(6,190m)

② **Logan**
19,550 ft.
(5,959m)

③ **Whitney**
14,504 ft.
(4,421m)

④ **Popocatépetl**
17,930 ft.
(5,465m)

⑤ **Cotopaxi**
19,347 ft.
(5,897m)

⑥ **Aconcagua**
22,835 ft.
(6,960m)

⑦ **Kilimanjaro**
19,340 ft.
(5,895m)

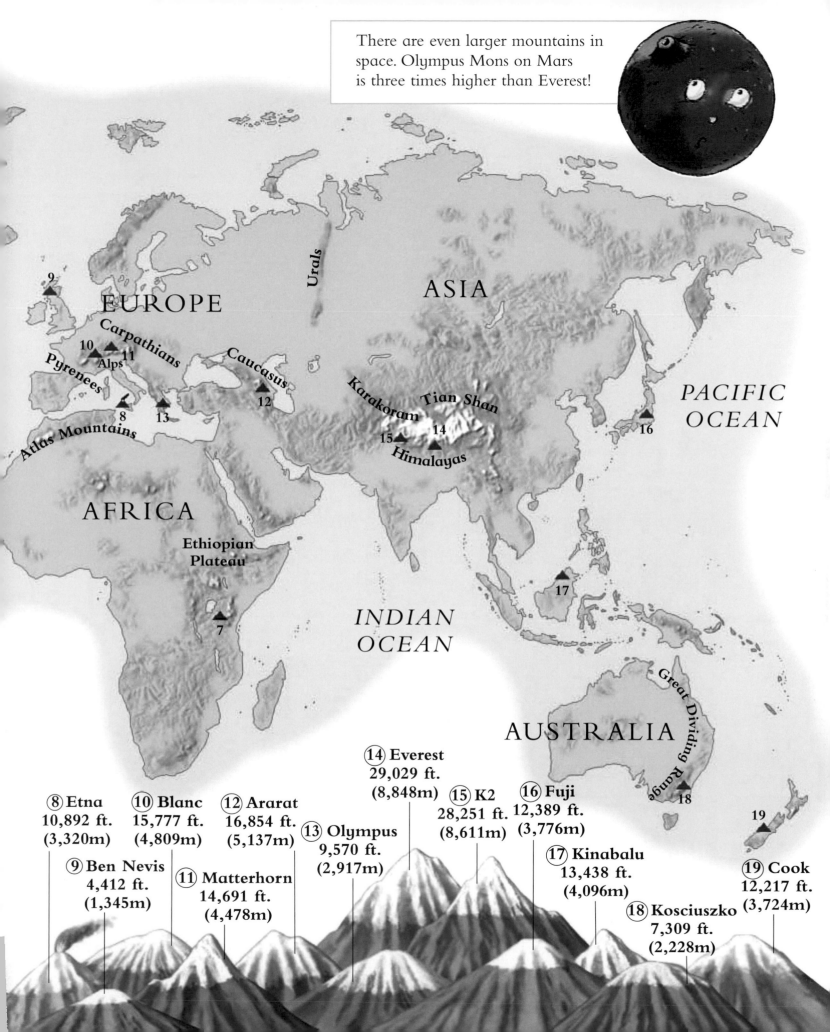

There are even larger mountains in space. Olympus Mons on Mars is three times higher than Everest!

URALS

ASIA

EUROPE

Carpathians

Caucasus

Tian Shan

PACIFIC OCEAN

10 11
Alps

Pyrenees

Karakoram

Atlas Mountains

8 13

12

15 14
Himalayas

9

AFRICA

Ethiopian Plateau

16

INDIAN OCEAN

17

7

AUSTRALIA

Great Dividing Range

18

19

⑧ Etna
10,892 ft.
(3,320m)

⑩ Blanc
15,777 ft.
(4,809m)

⑫ Ararat
16,854 ft.
(5,137m)

⑭ Everest
29,029 ft.
(8,848m)

⑮ K2
28,251 ft.
(8,611m)

⑯ Fuji
12,389 ft.
(3,776m)

⑬ Olympus
9,570 ft.
(2,917m)

⑨ Ben Nevis
4,412 ft.
(1,345m)

⑪ Matterhorn
14,691 ft.
(4,478m)

⑰ Kinabalu
13,438 ft.
(4,096m)

⑲ Cook
12,217 ft.
(3,724m)

⑱ Kosciuszko
7,309 ft.
(2,228m)

Do mountains move?

Crust

Mantle

Core

They certainly do! Earth is a little like a giant round egg, with a shell called the crust, then a layer called the mantle, and then a core in the middle. The crust is cracked, like an eggshell made from 30 or so gigantic pieces called plates. The plates float around very slowly on top of the mantle, which is fluid, a little like molasses.

The plates that carry North America and Europe are floating apart by about 1.5 inches (4cm) each year.

How do mountains form?

Volcanoes are openings in the crust where fiery clouds of hot ash, gas, and red-hot runny rock, called lava, spit out. Most volcanic mountains form as lava and ash cool into layer upon layer of solid rock.

Although the plates that make up Earth's crust move very slowly, their movements are powerful enough to make mountains. Different movements give birth to the three main types of mountains—volcanic, block, and fold.

Why do some mountains have pointed tops?

Even while a mountain is forming, the weather, ice, and running water start to wear it away and carve its top into sharp points. This wearing away is called erosion.

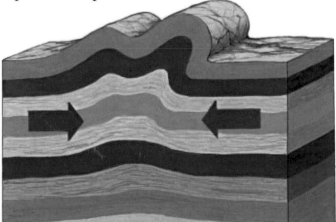

Wind carries grit and sand, which work like sandpaper, slowly rubbing rocks away.

Block mountains form when part of the crust is squeezed up between two cracks called faults.

Fold mountains form as two plates slowly crunch into each other, pushing the crust up into bumps and folds.

Why do volcanoes blow their tops?

A volcano begins deep inside Earth as bubbles of gas and liquid rock called magma. This mixture slowly rises because it is lighter than the solid rock around it. As it pushes its way up, it gets squashed and squeezed. The pressure builds up and up, until the gas and magma explode through a weak place in Earth's crust—making the volcano erupt and blow its top.

The effect of gas and magma erupting from a volcano is a little like what happens when you shake a soda bottle and then take off the cap.

When magma reaches the surface, it is called lava.

Are all volcanoes dangerous?

The ancient Romans believed that a god of fire lived beneath a volcanic island off the Italian coast. They called the god Vulcanus—and that's where our word *volcano* comes from.

There are three main types of volcanoes, and they can all be dangerous. Active volcanoes erupt fairly often. Dormant volcanoes have been sleeping quietly for years but may erupt again one day. Extinct volcanoes have stopped erupting and are unlikely to erupt again—if we're lucky!

Sometimes magma and gases explode through side tunnels called vents.

Which was the noisiest volcano?

When Indonesia's Krakatau blew its top in 1883, the roar of the explosion was heard more than one-eighth of the way around the world— as far away as Sri Lanka, the Philippines, and central Australia.

Which mountains grow into islands?

There are thousands of tiny islands dotted throughout the world's oceans, and most of them were made by volcanoes slowly growing up from the ocean floor.

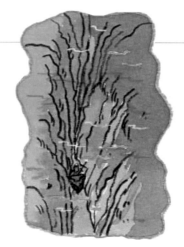

With its bottom 35,994 feet (10,971m) below sea level, the world's deepest valley is the Marianas Trench in the Pacific Ocean.

The world's longest mountain range is almost completely underwater. It's called the Mid-Atlantic Ridge, and it stretches for about 9,900 miles (16,000km), from Iceland almost to Antarctica.

Mid-Atlantic Ridge

NORTH AMERICA

EUROPE

AFRICA

SOUTH AMERICA

ATLANTIC OCEAN

Can mountains sink?

Yes—an atoll is a ring-shaped island that can form around the rim of a sunken volcano. An atoll is made from limestone, and the limestone is made by tiny sea creatures called coral polyps.

Lagoon   **Coral atoll**

The water in the middle of a coral atoll is called a lagoon.

What are black smokers?

Black smokers are strange chimney stacks that build up on the ocean floor and belch out steamy black clouds of boiling hot water. All kinds of weird and wonderful animals live near them, including red-and-white worms as long as cars.

Why do mountains have snow on top?

Not all mountains have snow on top—only the highest ones do. That's because when water gets very cold, it freezes and turns into snow or ice—and the higher you go up a mountain, the colder it gets. The place where a mountain begins to be covered in snow is called the snow line.

The higher you go up a mountain, the windier it gets. Winds can howl at more than 190 miles per hour (300km/h) at the top of the Himalayas.

For every 1,000 feet (300m) you climb up a mountain, the temperature drops by about 3.5°F (2°C).

When does snow move as fast as a racecar?

Sometimes on high mountains, a mass of snow slips suddenly and begins to slide downhill. This is an avalanche. The worst avalanches hurtle downward like racecars, at more than 100 miles per hour (160km/h).

Can snow move mountains?

Snow and ice can crack and break rocks, slowly wearing away mountains. The most powerful mountain movers are glaciers. These massive blocks of ice, snow, and rock form high up in mountains and flow downhill like vast frozen rivers, carving out valleys.

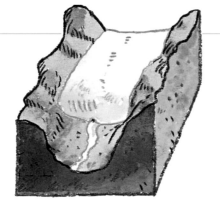

Glaciers carve out U-shaped valleys. V-shaped valleys are formed by rivers.

Glacier

Why don't plants grow on mountaintops?

The top of a high mountain is one of the coldest, windiest places on Earth, and plants hate it there. Plants need water, sunlight, and soil that they can get their roots into. Take these things away and plants give up and die.

Rivers and melting snow wash soil down from mountaintops, so the higher up you go, the thinner the soil is.

Which plants grow on mountainsides?

Large trees can't survive up near the snow line, but alpines are small, ground-hugging plants that have developed ways of beating the poor soil and bad weather.

The world's oldest-known tree lives in Dalarna, Sweden. It's a spruce, and it has already had 9,550 birthdays!

How do mountain plants keep warm?

Some alpine plants, such as edelweiss, have hairy leaves that work like an animal's furry coat to keep them warm. Others, such as gentians, have very dark leaves and flowers, because dark colors attract more of the Sun's warmth than light colors do.

Plants can't take in water if it is frozen as ice or snow.

The toughest kinds of trees are conifers such as pine trees, but even they cannot grow on high slopes.

Which plant can melt snow?

Like many plants, the alpine snowbell disappears underground in the winter. When new shoots start to push up through the snow in the spring, they give off enough heat to melt their way through.

Can animals live on mountains?

Animals find mountain life just as tough as plants do, so most of them stick to the lower slopes. The ones that live higher up have to be good climbers, such as mountain sheep, goats, and antelope.

The Rocky Mountain goat can climb the steepest cliffs. Hollows under its hooves stick on rocks like suction cups to keep it from slipping.

Which mountain animal has a skirt?

The yak's long, silky hair falls into a skirt around its knees, keeping it warm. This is just as well, as it lives in the highest region in the world—Tibet, in Asia.

How high do birds nest?

Although many birds make flying visits, very few nest high up in the mountains. The record holder is the alpine chough, which nests as high on the slopes as 23,000 feet (7,000m).

The Andean condor spends its days soaring above the Andes Mountains of South America. Its wings are wide enough for a car to park on!

Which animal became famous for mountain rescues?

Some people believe that big, hairy, apelike creatures called yetis live in the Himalayas. However, no one has ever proved that yetis really exist.

Saint Bernards are big, smart dogs that are famous for rescuing travelers who have lost their way in snowy mountain passes. The dogs were first trained back in the 1600s by monks living in the Alps.

Why do mountain houses have sloping roofs?

A sloping roof stops too much snow from piling up on top of a mountain house—the extra snow slides off, like a skier sliding down a slope. The parts of the roof that stick out beyond the walls are very wide, too, to keep the falling snow away from the walls.

Why do farmers build steps on mountains?

In many parts of the world, mountain farmers build low walls to keep rainwater from washing away the soil. This creates stepped fields, called terraces, where the soil is deep enough for crops to grow.

Lake Titicaca is too high for many trees to grow there, so everything from boats to houses is made out of reeds.

Who fishes on the world's highest lake?

At more than 12,500 feet (3,800m) above sea level, Lake Titicaca in Peru is the highest navigable lake in the world. Local people live on islands in the lake and fish from boats woven from reeds.

If you don't want to build a house on a mountain, you can always live in a cave. For thousands of years, the people of Cappadocia, Turkey, have tunneled homes in weird chimneys of volcanic rock.

Some mountain rivers are blocked and turned into lakes by a strong high wall called a dam. The lake water is used to power machines that generate electricity.

Who built palaces in the mountains?

Back in the 1400s, the Inca ruled over vast parts of the Andes Mountains of South America. They built amazing stone towns and palaces in the mountains, including the mysterious Machu Picchu.

The Inca were conquered by Spanish invaders in the 1500s. When American explorer Hiram Bingham stumbled across Machu Picchu in 1911, it had been deserted for well over 400 years.

Which monks live in the mountains?

Mount Athos in Greece is home to 20 monasteries—and many, many monks. It isn't a single peak. It is a mountainous strip of land that sticks out like a finger from the mainland.

Which city is on top of the world?

Tibet borders the Himalayas, and it's so high that people call it the "roof of the world." It's no surprise, then, that the Tibetan city of Lhasa is the world's highest, at 11,975 feet (3,650m) above sea level.

Even valley bottoms in Tibet are higher than most countries' mountains.

Who were the mountain men?

Women aren't allowed to visit Mount Athos— even female animals are banned!

American explorers such as Kit Carson became known as mountain men during the 1800s because they roamed through the wildest parts of the Rocky Mountains, trapping beavers and other animals for their fur.

When did the first person climb a mountain?

Although people must have been scrambling up high mountains for thousands of years, we only know about the climbers whose stories have been recorded in writing. One of the first recorded high climbs took place in A.D. 633, when a Japanese monk named En no Shokaku made it to the top of Mount Fuji.

One of the first rock climbers on record was a Roman soldier. In 106 B.C., he scaled a steep cliff face hunting for rock snails to eat—and discovered a path that the rest of the army then used to make a surprise attack on an enemy camp.

Who were the first people to climb Mount Everest?

The first people to climb the world's highest mountain were Edmund Hillary of New Zealand and Tenzing Norgay of Nepal. They reached the summit of Everest on May 29, 1953.

How do people climb mountains?

Climbers use special equipment to help them get up steep rock faces and over slippery ground and to protect them from falls. Ropes are a climber's lifeline—one end goes around the waist, and the other is looped through metal spikes called pitons, which are hammered into the rock as the climber moves upward.

To get a grip on slippery snow and ice, climbers attach metal spikes called crampons to their boots.

The first woman to get to the top of Mount Everest was Junko Tabei of Japan, on May 16, 1975.

How do people surf on snow?

People have been sliding along on skis for thousands of years—someone scratched a picture of a skier on a rock in Norway more than 10,000 years ago.

They head for the mountains with a snowboard! Snowboards are a cross between a ski, a surfboard, and a wheelless skateboard. When they were first made in the 1960s, they were called "Snurfers."

Eager snowboarders don't give up when spring comes and the snow melts. They just switch to a new kind of souped-up skateboard— a mountain board.

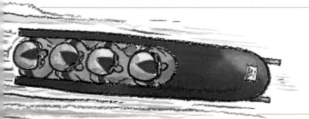

Bobsleds are the racecars of the Winter Olympics. Teams of two or four riders jump in wearing crash helmets and race down icy runways at speeds of up to 100 miles per hour (160km/h).

Who hurtles down mountains like an express train?

High-speed trains can zip along at up to 430 miles per hour (690km/h), and speed skiers and snowboarders are not far behind. The world speed-skiing record is just over 158 miles per hour (255km/h).

Which bike climbs mountains?

A mountain bike has several gears to help you pedal up steep tracks, and knobby tires for gripping slippery slopes. And if the going gets too tough, you can always get off and carry the bike!

Which is the longest mountain tunnel?

Switzerland is home to one of the world's longest rail tunnels. The Gotthard Base Tunnel burrows for more than 35 miles (57km) through the Alps. It runs almost 1 and a half miles under the mountain at its deepest point.

More than 2,000 years ago, a general named Hannibal led an army and 40 shivering African war elephants over the Alps to attack Rome.

Where is the world's highest railroad?

The Qingzang railroad between China and the region of Tibet crosses the Himalaya Mountains, climbing to about 16,640 feet (5,072m) above sea level. As the train travels through the higher mountains, the air becomes very thin, so passengers are given oxygen to help them breathe.

To keep them from slipping backward, the wheels on some mountain trains come in threes instead of the usual twos. The third wheel is in the middle and is toothed so that it hooks onto a racked track.

Which is the steepest railroad?

The world's longest cable car line is in Vietnam. It runs for almost 4 miles (6.3km), taking tourists from Muong Hoa Valley to the peak of Fansipan Mountain.

The view is fantastic on the Katoomba Scenic Railway in Australia's Blue Mountains, but the ride is pretty hairy. This railroad is the world's steepest, dropping 1,360 feet (415m) in a little under two minutes.

Where is the "great pebble"?

The world's largest rock is a special place for the Aboriginal people of central Australia, who call it Uluru, meaning "great pebble." Uluru soars almost 1,142 feet (348m) above the surrounding desert and measures 5 miles (8km) around its base.

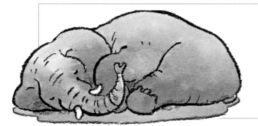

Uluru glows a bright red when sunlight hits it at dawn and dusk. When the sky is cloudy, it looks like the back of a huge sleeping elephant.

Why do people climb Mount Fuji?

At 12,389 feet (3,776m), Mount Fuji is the highest mountain in Japan and one of the world's most famous mountains. It's also one of Japan's holiest places—more than half a million people climb it every year to say their prayers on its summit.

The ancient Greeks believed that Zeus, the king of their gods, lived in a glittering palace on top of Mount Olympus. Olympus rises to 9,570 feet (2,917m) and is the highest mountain in Greece.

Which mountain looks like a tabletop?

Table Mountain in South Africa was named because its summit is as flat as a tabletop. It is often covered in clouds, which people call the "tablecloth."

Africa's highest mountain is Kilimanjaro. At 19,340 feet (5,895m), Kilimanjaro is so high that its top is always covered by snow and ice—even though it's in hot lands close to the equator.

Index